About the Author

Dana Brown Smith is a hands-on, feet-to-the-fire advocate for freedom from fascination with pornography. Drawing on her own personal involvement with porn and her professional experience as an expert in investigating and responding to sexual harassment claims in the workplace, she brings an in-depth and well-rounded perspective to the conversation on the effect of pornography, especially as it relates to women.

In addition to being a frequent blogger on Huffington Post, Dana volunteers around the world serving those in need of basic living assistance. She works, writes, and lives in Los Angeles, a stone's throw from the epicenter of America's porn industry.

Do you think you're alone when it comes to being fascinated with pornography? You're not. Dana Brown Smith is standing proudly next to you. She's made the journey through fascination with porn.

The change came when she became aware that what started as simple titillation turned into more. She saw that women who viewed sexually explicit materials were ingesting images that promoted sexually deviant behavior and de-emphasized the belief in love, commitment, marriage, and family. As these realizations awakened, she looked for, found, and implemented methods for regaining control of her choices and her life. She did it consciously and deliberately—and what she learned can assist you, whether you're just feeling guilty (she'll assure you that's not necessary), or you're feeling trapped.

In *Girls Watch Too!* you will discover:

- How familiarity breeds emulation when consuming pornography
- The unintended and not-so-pleasant effects of pornography consumption on romantic relationships
- How to identify and manage those "triggers" that lead to the desire to watch pornography
- Ways to recognize and/or prevent teenage porn consumption with your children
- Techniques for creating a climate of compassion if your spouse is struggling with porn

- Methods for recognizing and overcoming a porn habit *without judgment or condemnation*

Filled with entertaining anecdotes, the book tackles a variety of issues ranging from the accessibility of porn, the business of porn, and the emergence of porn in the workplace to the influence of sexually explicit materials on our pop culture, cell phones, video games and social networking sites. It is solidly based on a foundation of experience and proven effective techniques. And in the unique bonus section you will learn how to utilize uplifting spiritual and scriptural tools and strategies to discourage porn consumption and maintain porn abstinence.

Far from a serious, clinical text, the tone is warm and conversational and tackles a difficult subject in an honest and non-judgmental way so that any woman who watches pornography can break free of the compulsion it may have over them.

Girls watch too!

Female Fascination with Porn: Why You Should Care and What You Can Do About It

Girls watch too!

Dana Brown Smith

Bellflower, CA

Exalted Publishing
15545 Bellflower Blvd., Ste. C,
Bellflower, CA 90706

Printed in the United States of America

Publisher's Cataloguing-in-Publication Data

Smith, Dana Brown.

Girls watch too! : female fascination with porn -- why you should care and what you can do about it / Dana Brown Smith. -- First edition. -- Bellflower, CA : Exalted Publishing, 2015.

pages ; cm.

ISBN: 978-0-9864185-1-8 (trade) ; 978-0-9864185-0-1 (ebook)

Summary: Research shows that women are viewing pornography at a rapidly increasing rate. If you are among women who watch and are concerned--even alarmed--that you can't stop, in "Girls Watch Too!" you will find hope ... and help. Coming from the experience, mind and heart of a woman who was caught in a fascination with porn, the book challenges traditional thinking of guilt, shame and condemnation. If you would like to step free, you will find a practical path of psychological, emotional and, in the bonus section, scriptural/spiritual techniques to doing just that.--Publisher.

1. Women and erotica. 2. Women--Sexual behavior. 3. Women --Psychology. 4. Pornography--Psychological aspects. 5. Pornographic films--Psychological aspects. 6. Internet pornography--Psychological aspects. 7. Sex (Psychology) 8. Sex addiction--Treatment. 9. Sex addicts--Rehabilitation. 10. Self-help techniques. 11. Self-help techniques--Religious aspects. 12. Sex addiction--Treatment--Religious aspects. I. Title. II. Title: Female fascination with porn.

HQ471 .S65 2015 2015900674
363.4/7--dc23 1502

Book Consultant: Ellen Reid
Cover Design: Lisa Hainline
Interior Design: Ghislain Viau

To my critique group:
Thank you for your feedback, encouragement
and unwavering support.

Table of Contents

Introduction

Not long ago I attended a business networking meeting. You know those groups where you meet for breakfast and share leads with other professionals in your industry? This particular morning I was visiting with a new chapter and everyone was asked to introduce themselves, their businesses, and share with the group something that others might not know about them. I could sense the excitement as this group of high achievers regaled the room with stories of their extreme hobbies, exotic travels, and personal accomplishments.

As the introductions made their way toward my side of the room, I quickly sifted through my mental Rolodex of interesting facts. What could I say that would be memorable to the group? I could share that I've traveled to multiple international destinations as a short-term missionary, but others had already talked about their extensive travel experiences. I could share that I've run a half-marathon, but someone else had already proclaimed this accomplishment—and for a full marathon, no less.

Shaken from my thoughts, the meeting host motioned for me to stand and face the room. Still undecided about what I would say, I quickly bounced up out of my seat to address the group. Before I could catch myself, I blurted out in an excited tone, "I'm passionate about porn!" Everyone in the room stared at me in suspended animation for what seemed like an eternity until someone yelled, "Yes!" and started to clap. At this point the room erupted into laughter. After the group settled down, I went on to explain that I'm passionate about those who struggle with pornography compulsions, particularly women.

What I didn't share that day was that I've had my own personal struggles with pornography consumption, hooked on its intoxicating images and themes. As a woman of faith, I struggled with a duplicitous lifestyle, torn between doing what I was raised to believe was right, but unable to resist what I felt spiritually was wrong. It's been over five years since I kicked the porn habit. Before my turning point, I hid my habit in silence. Now, I'm compelled to not only share my story, but to present a different perspective on this very important issue.

And so I've written this book. However, this is *not* a clinical study of the effects of pornography consumption, nor is it a discussion of the impact molestation or rape has on a woman's sexual thoughts, patterns, or behaviors. While these are crucial aspects of pornography compulsions, I simply do not have the expertise or personal experience to address them. If that is what you're looking for, there are some outstanding resources available on these subjects. In fact, I've listed them in the appendix.

Instead, I wrote this book because I noticed something intriguing from my experiences with women who I know personally and those I know indirectly. Women of all walks of life and faith are consuming pornography at increased levels. As I began to research this phenomenon, I learned that there are a variety of reasons why porn and erotica are on the rise. Many do it as a means of self-stimulation, to indulge a fetish, or because they feel it will improve their performance in the bedroom. For some, the desire to connect with pornography is birthed out of a past sexual abuse; for others it's a form of entertainment, just like watching a sitcom or reality TV show.

Whatever the impetus, female pornography consumption is trending. And even with the negative themes often portrayed in pornography such as a de-emphasis on commitment and marriage, as well as the objectification of women, I still encountered story after story of women viewing and reading sexually explicit material. And for those whose connection to porn had become compulsive, I found that there are limited resources available to assist them with changing their behavior.

So here it is: a non-confrontational and non-judgmental exploration of female pornography consumption. In this book we're going to look at pornography from a woman's point of view. We'll explore its accessibility, the impact it has on our relationships and families, and its emotional and spiritual effects. I'll even provide tools and strategies to break a porn habit for those interested.

This book was written for women who are struggling with porn and want to stop. This book was also written for women who are actively engaged with porn and have no desire to stop. And if you're thinking, *I don't watch porn,* or *I'm not a woman,* but you *are* interested in this topic, by all means, continue reading! ■

Chapter One

Handbags, Belts, and Porn, Oh My!

There was something mysterious about the black box my parents brought home and attached to our 1970's television set. To the delight of me and my friends, we were one of the first families in the neighborhood to have what was called "ON TV." With this amazing new invention, we could watch movies without commercial interruption. And not just the old films played on the major networks. No, this was the good stuff—movies that had recently been shown at the drive-in theater. It was as if our television set had received a major overhaul.

It didn't take long for me and my friends to discover that certain channels were blocked. After some investigation, we realized that one of those channels showed peculiar images late at night. Though there was no sound, if we watched intently through the fuzz, snow, and big squiggly lines, we could make out the body parts of men and women playing a strange game of Twister with no clothes on. This was my first exposure to pornography.

The dictionary defines *pornography* as "the depiction of erotic behavior intended to cause sexual excitement."[1] This is a broad definition. More specifically, pornography includes forms of books, art, pictures, magazines, and video. It can be soft-core (mostly foreplay and erotic storyline with simulated sexual intercourse) or hard-core (graphic depictions of sex acts with sexual penetration). Pornography has many genres, such as bondage, voyeurism, and exhibitionism; it often depicts a wide variety of sexual partners, including sex between men and women, men and men, women and women, group sex, sex with strangers, and sex with forbidden partners.

Pornography is easy to access via magazines, books, cable/satellite TV, and the big kahuna—the Internet. It's also found in unlikely places such as video games, online social-networking communities, workplace computers, and even cell phones. Consider the following: Each year, I get together with a group of friends I've known since childhood for a Christmas luncheon. I love the excited laughter, warm hugs, and sharing family photos.

On one particularly year, we were all dressed to impress, and my friend Taylor was no exception as she showed off an exquisite belt crafted from hand-cut glass, fastened together with a jewel-encrusted band (with a price tag equivalent to one month's rent for a two-bedroom apartment). However, the showstopper for me was not Taylor's bling-bling belt, but the surprise that our friend Jamie shared with us on her cell phone. Here we were in an upscale restaurant huddled around a tiny screen trying to make out the grainy images in a twenty-second video. Even in low resolution, it was obviously porn. Although we all erupted in a fit of laughter, I wondered, *Do lots of women carry sexually explicit materials on their phones just like pictures of their children?* No longer limited to desktop computers or television, these days porn is carried around in pockets, backpacks... even in Louis Vuitton handbags.

Pornography is big business. Producers of porn websites are making hefty sums, oftentimes with little overhead and small start-up capital. To make a profit, some sites charge a nominal subscription fee to view content; however, others offer their content for free and rely on the heavy traffic to generate advertising dollars.

Revenues generated by the adult entertainment industry are difficult to calculate and include earnings from the Internet, adult video sales, adult video rentals, pay-per-view, cable/satellite TV, mobile phone sex, exotic dance clubs, sex toys/novelties, and magazines. Big hoteliers are also making huge profits from porn with guests who purchase in-room sexually explicit movies. While numerous articles estimate annual industry revenues of between ten and thirteen million dollars during the mid-2000s, it's difficult to identify the source of those figures. How much capital does the industry truly generate? It's hard to tell; however, as free online content continues to rise in popularity, coupled with the rise in Internet piracy of professionally produced adult videos, estimated annual industry revenues have and will continue to fall.

As pornography grows in popularity, its impact reaches multiple demographics and age groups. In a 2006 study of 563 college students, 72.8 percent of participants had seen online pornography before age 18, with most exposure beginning between the ages of 14 to 17. While it's difficult to generalize the results of this study, researchers do suggest that if student responses are typical, a young person's exposure to porn is a normative experience.[2] In a 2014 national survey conducted by the Barna Group, 2 out of 10 women aged 18 to 30 report viewing pornography at least monthly while women aged 30 to 41 are viewing at an increased rate of 42 percent.[3]

Over the years, the U.S. Congress has made many attempts to block distribution of and access to sexually explicit materials. The Comstock Act of 1873 made it a crime to circulate obscene literature and articles of immoral use.[4] In 1970, the federal government appointed the Lockhart Commission to study the effects of obscene material on violent behavior. While the results of the study affirmed the belief that pornography should not be sold to children, the commission found no link between pornography, crime, or delinquent activities in adults or youths; they therefore recommended the relaxation of legal restrictions on the use of all mediums of pornography.[5]

Sixteen years later, the Meese Commission released an exhaustive report concluding the opposite of the 1970 study and found that substantial exposure to degrading pornography can lead to conduct that is sexually violent, aggressive, and/or coercive.[6]

Pornographic films (and non-sexual movies, too) can depict dangerous and offensive themes. Take, for instance, content created by the now defunct production company Extreme Associates that depict naïve preteen girls being convinced to have sex with adult men. Or consider the psycho-slasher flick that portrays women being raped, strangled, suffocated, beaten, and urinated on. Another film is alleged to contain a scene in which Jesus Christ steps off the cross to have sex with an angel.[7]

So, is pornography an evil, insidious plague that is rapidly infecting our society? Or is it primarily entertainment for consenting adults, having little to no significant impact on relationships and marriages? There's no denying that pornography is a very powerful medium capable of shaping our attitudes and behaviors about sex. In the next chapter we'll explore this further and discuss the unlikely places that porn may be found, its accessibility, and how it's influencing the workplace. ■

Endnotes

1. *Merriam-Webster Online,* s.v. "pornography," accessed December 20, 2014, http://www.merriam-webster.com/dictionary/pornography

2. Chiara Sabina, Janis Wolak, and David Finkelhor, "The Nature and Dynamics of Internet Pornography Exposure for Youth," *CyberPsychology & Behavior,* December 2008, 11(6): 691-693. doi:10.1089/cpb.2007.0179.

3. The website of the Proven Men Ministry, "2014 Porn Survey," Barna Group, accessed December 20, 2014, http://www.provenmen.org/2014pornsurvey/

4. *Encyclopedia Britannica Online,* s.v. "Comstock Act," accessed December 21, 2014, http://www.britannica.com/EBcheckedltopic/130734/Comstock-Act

5. Donald Downs, "The Attorney General's Commission and the New Politics of Pornography," *American Bar Foundation Research Journal,* 12 (Autumn, 1987), 639, 641-679, http://www.jstor.org/stable/828375

6. Ibid.

7. Dan Kennedy, "Holy War," *The Boston Phoenix,* September 5–11, 2003, http://www.bostonphoenix.com/

Chapter Two

Fancy Meeting You Here

One night a group of workout buddies and I went out for a meal. If you're into group exercise at a fitness club, you know it's common to see the same faces at the gym. What begins as a nod or a smile turns into a great conversation about nutrition, and dishing about the instructors. Soon you're saving a space for each other in workout classes, providing encouragement to eat healthy, and even spending time together on the weekends.

This particular night, we were all feeling good after a strenuous workout when I told my friends I was writing a book about pornography. I chuckled to myself as out of the corner of my eye I caught our male instructor, who typically appears bored with the banter between us ladies, perk up with my revelation. We launched into a spirited debate about what's considered pornography and the pros and cons of watching sexually explicit material.

Then Angie—workout buddy and gal pal—shared an encounter she had. "I was supposed to hang out with one of my girls at her house. When I got there, she wasn't home, but this fine-looking man was standing outside the house next door."

We all laughed at Angie's emphasis on the word *fine*. My fitness instructor rolled his eyes.

"So ya'll know me, being the sociable person I am, I just *had* to go up to this brotha' and introduce myself. So we're vibin', having a cool conversation, and I ask him what he does for a living. And gurrrl, this man told me that he is a porn star."

"What?" we all said collectively, waiting anxiously for Angie to finish.

"He sure did. He said it just like you tell someone you work at a grocery store or at the bank. Then he said he was running late to go film a porn video."

I don't know if it was the endorphins generated by our workout or the sugary drinks so late at night, but we all doubled over with laughter and screams.

Angie went on to tell us that she talked with the fine man for almost twenty minutes while he waited for his ride. When no one showed up, Angie agreed to drive him to his film shoot. Again, the table erupted as we all called her crazy for letting this gorgeous stranger in her car. A coy grin began to emerge across my instructor's face, who by this time was fully engaged in Angie's story.

"I expected the place to be at a glamorous Hollywood studio, with lots of cameras and those trailers you see when someone's filming a movie. But we pulled up to a small house in a nice neighborhood. People were walking their dogs and kids were playing right there in the street."

"What happened next?" I asked, on the edge of my seat.

"When he got out of my car, he asked if I wanted to go in and meet some of the people."

"You watched them shoot a porno?" one of the ladies blurted out.

"No, no, I'm not that freaky. I was definitely curious, but naw. I just said good-bye and left."

While everyone at the table continued to interrogate Angie about her encounter, I pondered what might have happened if she had gone into the house. Would there be others like her, standing around observing the action? When did it become normal to watch people have sex like Monday night football or your local eleven o'clock news?

Many people are watching sex, and how we access porn has evolved over time. From magazines to adult theaters; from VCRs to DVDs; from the Internet to mobile phones—each technological advancement has made sexually explicit materials more accessible.

More Americans are watching video on smartphones too. Enhancements in cellular connectivity speeds (faster phone speed equals better video viewing quality) and the rise in unlimited data plans allow for easy consumption of mobile adult content. Combine that with the proliferation of mobile phones (the United Nations reports that more people have access to mobile phones than toilets)[1] and the development of new apps, and you've got porn that's more convenient than a public restroom.

Although a phone's screen size is much smaller than a computer monitor or television set, users can view mobile porn more privately by using headphones to reduce the likelihood of detection when others are nearby. Soccer moms are discreetly viewing porn while waiting in the stands at their children's practices, and teens are camouflaging porn use as their parents sit nearby in the living room. It's more difficult to conceal porn use on a thirty-two-inch television screen or a twenty-inch computer monitor than on a five-inch, handheld, cell phone screen.

Pornography is heavily consumed from the Internet, whether from a mobile device or computer. The Internet is home to numerous web pages that contain sexually explicit material, and 13 percent of all searches relate to some form of erotic content.[2] Twenty years ago, if you wanted to view sexually explicit materials, you needed to go to an adult video store or purchase an adult entertainment channel on cable television. Now you can surf the web and find pornography whether you're looking for it or not. Of the one million most popular websites, at least 42,337 are sexually explicit.[3]

Not only are people watching pornography on the Internet, they're doing so, surprisingly, during working hours. Employees engage in non-work-related activities while on the clock. A Salary.com survey found that 64 percent of workers admit to cyber-slacking, spending anywhere between one and ten hours per week using office computers for personal activities such as social networking and, yes, watching pornography.[4,5]

Cyber-slacking can be expensive for employers, especially during the month of March, when the NCAA basketball finals take place. From Sweet Sixteen to the Final Four, March Madness has become a beloved office pastime for many employees, costing employers precious hours of lost productivity. A report released by CareerBuilder.com estimates that one in five workers has historically engaged in March Madness activities, and these are not just entry-level or administrative employees; 33 percent of management employees whose annual salary exceeds $100,000 are likely to participate in workplace wagers compared to 14 percent of lower-wage earners.[6]

Cyber-slacking is not limited to March Madness antics, but it includes employees who are viewing sexually explicit materials right under their bosses' noses, much to the dismay (or enjoyment) of their cubical mates. Nearly two-thirds of U.S. adult men (63 percent) admit to having looked at pornography at least one time over a three-month period while at work, and more than one-third of U.S. women (36 percent) admit to viewing pornography at least one time over a three-month period while at work.[7]

Unlike March Madness, accessing porn during business hours (whether on a company computer or a personal mobile device) is not limited to a few weeks during the year. This activity occurs in offices across the nation each business day of the year. Lost productivity and employee terminations are just a few pitfalls. Watching pornography on the company computer is typically grounds for disciplinary action. If your employer has an IT department, they're most likely monitoring your every move on the Internet. (There's software designed to do just that.) When you visit a site that violates the Internet usage policy, you may be marched into the HR department with some explaining to do.

Work computers that repeatedly get infected with viruses are often a dead giveaway that an employee is accessing pornography. The IT rep then starts digging around in your system, looking for signs that you're viewing porn while you're on the clock.

Some employees have learned to bypass internal monitoring systems. Here are just a few ways workers are hiding their porn stash:[8]

- Importing pornographic images into spreadsheets and .pdf files
- Clearing the browser history of all pornography websites
- Renaming sexually explicit files to appear as though they're work-related
- Saving all pornography images in one computer folder so the entire file can be deleted in one easy keystroke
- Changing folder properties to "hide" so that sexually explicit materials cannot be discovered
- Disabling the operating system history so that pornographic files don't show up in the Windows start menu under "Most Recent Documents"

Porn consumption at work can lead to other personnel headaches, including employee grievances. Consider the following sexual harassment claim filed by a female employee named Violet against her male co-worker Jason. In Violet's complaint, she alleged that Jason, with whom she shared a cubicle, was watching pornography throughout the day. While Jason never asked her to participate in his viewing pleasures, Violet was offended by the images on his computer. He didn't make any sexual advances toward her. He never shared the details of his sex life with her, nor did he ask about her sex life. He did not touch her inappropriately. But because Violet had an unobstructed view of his screen, and because Jason watched porn at work, he inadvertently created an environment that was sexually charged and offensive to her. She became distracted and unable to complete her work assignments effectively. When Jason was questioned about his actions, his response was that he never intended to offend Violet. However, in sexual harassment claims, intent is irrelevant. Jason lost his job.

Why would someone take the chance of getting caught viewing porn at work? Some people don't have Internet access at home, and some may not have speedy browsing capability. Technology issues aside, one of the most common reasons people view pornography at work is that they have a strong attraction to sexually explicit materials and have lost the ability to limit their viewing to after business hours.

In the book *The Porn Trap*, researchers Wendy and Larry Maltz assert that when a person views pornography, the dopamine chemical is produced in the brain at dramatic levels, inducing a drug-like sensation similar to crack cocaine.[9] Additional "feel-good" chemicals are also formed, which reduce the body's ability to furnish quantities at normal levels in ordinary circumstance (e.g., kissing, intercourse, and foreplay), therefore causing the porn-addicted psyche to demand more and more sexually explicit materials to achieve satisfaction. The risks of embarrassment, shame, and potential loss of income are overlooked for another fix.

We've explored some nontraditional places where porn is accessed. In the next chapter we'll see how teens are impacted by sexually explicit materials and are actively engaging with pornography via text messages. ■

Endnotes

1. The website of the UN News Centre, "Deputy UN Chief Calls for Urgent Action to Tackle Global Sanitation Crisis," United Nations, accessed December 21, 2014, http://www.un.org/apps/news/

2. Sai Gaddam and Ogi Ogas, *A Billion Wicked Thoughts: What the Internet Tells Us About Sexual Relationships,* New York: Penguin Group 2011.

3. Ibid.

4. The website of Salary.com, "Why & How Your Employees are Wasting Time at Work," accessed December 23, 2014, http://business.salary.com/why-how-your-employees-are-wasting-time-at-work/

5. Wendy Maltz, LCSW, DST and Larry Maltz, LCSW, *The Porn Trap: The Essential Guide to Overcoming Problems Caused by Pornography,* New York: HarperCollins e-books, 2008.

6. The website of Careerbuilder.com, "One in Five Workers Participate in March madness office Pools, Finds Career-Builder Survey," accessed December 23, 2014, http://www.careerbuilder.com/share/aboutus/pressreleases/

7. The website of the Proven Men Ministry, "2014 Porn Survey," Barna Group, accessed December 20, 2014, http://www.provenmen.org/2014pornsurvey/

8. The website of eHow, "How to Hide a Hard Disk Porn Stash," accessed January 23, 2010, http://www.ehow.com/how_2054913_hide-hard-disk-porn-stash

9. Maltz and Maltz, *The Porn Trap.*

Chapter Three

My Kid's Watching What?!

I experienced my first sex education class in elementary school. As an impressionable child, I could hardly wait to learn how mommies and daddies made babies. Nothing could spoil the excitement and anticipation of that day—not even the heartbreak felt by my best friend, whose parents restricted her from participating.

Kids still have the same curiosity about sex like I did. But now they're learning about the birds and the bees from pornography. Internet security company McAfee conducted the Teen Internet Behavior study and found that 70 percent of teens admit to hiding their online behavior from their parents, and 32 percent of teens report having accessed pornography online.[1] As more teens receive their sex ed from the monitor of a computer or the screen of their smartphone, impressionable young minds begin to view porn's unrealistic and often sexually deviant themes as standard and commonplace. When they rely on porn to guide them through this critical time of adolescence, the importance of committed relationships is deemphasized while deviant sexual behaviors are glorified. Practices that may have been completely off limits to them, such as group sex and BDSM, instead are readily available and spark curiosity in the minds of our youth.

The accessibility and anonymity of pornography has made it a dangerous teacher for youngsters. The lessons they learn are not those that promote healthy sexual relationships between married couples. In pornography, people have casual and indiscriminate sex without protection and do not get STDs or become pregnant. This isn't reality, and it sends the wrong message to anyone who views pornography, especially teenagers who already believe they're invincible. Our kids are emulating these behaviors with dire consequences.

My friend Tracy, who has a son named Eli, shared the following revelation with me:

"I caught Eli watching porn on his computer..." Her voice trailed off as she waited for my reaction.

"Really?" I wasn't sure what to say next.

She continued, "Yeah, it's really bad. He had all kind of crap saved on the computer."

"Oh gosh," I said as I shook my head. It was hard for me to picture her son watching porn. He's a nice young man, polite, an excellent student, an amazing pianist, and he holds a leadership position in the youth ministry at their church.

"He's only in the sixth grade," she said.

If you're not talking to your children about sex, someone (or some video) will. Statistics show that 78 percent of men and 45 percent of women report their first exposure to pornographic material between the ages of 12 to 15.[2] As our kids grow into adolescents, they remain at risk of exposure to pornography, but in new ways, which include taking and texting their own nude photos.

Sexting, the sending and receiving of sexually explicit photos, images, or messages via mobile device, has quickly become a regular occurrence. In a study of Los Angeles high school students, research shows that 15 percent of kids with cell phone access are sexting.[3] Somehow this risqué pastime has mainstreamed into a warped rite of passage for many teens who request nude photos of one another to express their romantic interest. A throwing of the bait, if you will. It's a litmus test to gauge the interest of the other party, and it happens at one of the most vulnerable times in a young relationship where trust has not been fully established, but infatuation takes precedence over common sense.

Nude photos have a high potential of falling into the wrong hands, especially when they're exchanged so early, long before a monogamous commitment is established. Even if a couple firmly establishes themselves as boyfriend and girlfriend and develops a catalogue of each other's naked images, all bets are off if the relationship goes south, frequently leading to unauthorized distribution of the explicit pictures.

To protect themselves from this seemingly inevitable declaration of war, teens turn to an arsenal of apps that promise anonymity and ingenious ways to text sexual images without fear of public exposure. If you're a parent with teenagers, you should be aware of apps like SnapChat, which allow users to send images that can only be accessed one time prior to self-destruction. However, this doesn't prevent the recipient from capturing, archiving, and sharing a screen shot of the image before it disappears. On the other hand, Kik messaging app allows users to post images anonymously—one reason why the program has the reputation for catering to the sexting crowd.

The public distribution of private photos is not the only concern when it comes to sexting. In a 2011 study of Houston high school students, researchers found that teens who sexted by sending naked pictures of themselves were more likely to be sexually active the following year, as opposed to kids who were not actively sexting.[4] The study did not find any correlation between sexting and risky sexual behavior such as having sex with multiple partners, having sex without protection, and/or having sex while under the influence of a controlled substance. However, engaging in sex too early when the teen mind is not mature enough to understand the emotional and spiritual consequences of intercourse is dangerous.

In the first of its kind, researchers in Los Angeles, California, studied the sexting behaviors of middle school students ages 10 to 15. The study found that 20 percent of these teens (and tweens) receive sexually explicit text messages and identified a link between sexting and being sexually active.[5]

Summarily, both studies show that kids who are engaged in sexting are more likely to have sex, a troubling proposition. Teens are viewing pornographic images and it's leading to sexual encounters that they act out in real life, all at a young and impressionable age when it is difficult, if not impossible, to discern the emotional, physical, and spiritual complexities of becoming sexually active.

*****

Continuous pornography consumption creates a lasting impact, particularly in teens, and can lead to (1) a belief that deviant sexual behaviors are satisfying to all parties involved, (2) a belief that casual and anonymous sex is the norm, (3) a belief that abstinence and sexual inactivity are abnormal, and (4) a belief that commitment and marriage are sexually restrictive.

If you think your child would never watch pornography, I pray you're right. However, if there's even a remote chance that your kid might be watching porn (including sexting), take preventive measures.

If your kids have their own computer and/or TV, go into their room often to see what they're watching and what they're doing on the Internet. If you suspect that your children may be watching Internet porn, move the computer out of their room and into a public area like a family room.

Consider purchasing a software program to monitor your child's online activities. There are many to choose from, and they include such features as filtering unwanted online adult content and time-of-day (or night) control of Internet use. (Check the appendix for a list of accountability software applications.)

If your kids have access to cable or satellite, put a parental block on the adult channels and a time-of-day block on the movie channels. Remember to change your password from time to time, as teenagers are tech-savvy and can usually find ways to decipher your encryption.

When your kids have friends over, set house rules. Let your children and their guests know that you don't allow pornography in your house. Your son or daughter will be mortified, but that's okay. You're helping to prevent a future pornography habit for your child and maybe for their friends as well. Be bold with love. We want our kids to grow, develop, and think for themselves, but as long as they live with you, they have to obey your rules.

Don't forget about your teen's smartphone. Random phone checks are a great way to monitor your child's behavior. Although your son or daughter will definitely protest and resist handing you their phone, don't worry about invading their privacy. Your goal is not to snoop into every aspect of their wondrous world of teenage angst; rather, you simply want to check for signs of pornography use or inappropriate texting. Besides, most parents pay for their child's phone and/or service plan, so technically it's yours. Check the photo gallery and all messaging apps for sexually explicit images. Scan the text messages for acronyms like WTTP (want to trade pictures), GNOC (get naked on camera), and SUGARPIC (suggestive or erotic photo), which might signal that your child is engaged in risky sexual behavior.

Many teens have become masters at hiding their online activities. While random phone checks may not identify every questionable activity, it does provide an opportunity for you to talk with your son or daughter about pornography use and its rarely considered consequences.

Keep an open dialogue about pornography with your kids, even if those conversations make you uncomfortable.

You talk to your children about the dangers of drugs and alcohol, right? Tell them:

- People shown in pornography are actors, oftentimes with surgically enhanced bodies. Generally, women and men don't look like this, so don't compare your body to what you may have seen.
- In pornography, people do not use condoms. In real life, if you have unprotected sex, you are at high risk of getting pregnant or contracting a sexual transmitted disease.
- Sexting is a form of pornography production. You have no control over who the image may be sent to or where it might get posted. Don't send sexy or nude pictures of yourself to anyone.

Resist the urge to interrogate your child about pornography. Instead, open the conversation casually. Maybe you've seen your son or daughter posting suggestive pictures on Facebook, playing a video game with sexual content, or watching a cable channel that shows adult programming. Exploring these activities is a good way to open a discussion about pornography. Even if your child doesn't have much to say, that's fine. Porn abstinence shouldn't be a warning you give once and never revisit. Your goal is to start the dialogue and leave the door open for future communication on this issue.

In the next chapter we'll talk about the business of pornography and the experiences some women have had while working in the industry. ■

Endnotes

1. The website of McAfee, "McAfee Reveals What U.S. Teens are Really Doing Online, and How Little Their Parents Actually Know," accessed December 11, 2014, http://www.mcafee.com/us/about/news/2012/

2. The website of the Proven Men Ministry, "2014 Porn Survey," Barna Group, accessed December 20, 2014, http://www.provenmen.org/2014pornsurvey/

3. Eric Rice, Harmony Rhoades, Hailey Winetrobe, Monica Sanchez, Jorge Montoya, Aaron Plant and Timothy Kordic, "Sexually Explicit Cell Phone Messaging Associated With Sexual Risk Among Adolescents," *Pediatrics*, September 2012. doi:10.1542/peds.2012-0021.

4. Jeff R. Temple and HyeJeong Choi, "Longitudinal Association Between Teen Sexting and Sexual Behavior," *Pediatrics*, October 2014. DOI: 10.1542/peds.2014-1974.

5. Eric Rice, Jeremy Gibbs, Hailey Winetrobe, Harmony Rhoades, Aaron Plant, Jorge Montoya and Timothy Kordic, "Sexting and Sexual Behavior Among Middle School Students," *Pediatrics*, June 2014. 134; e21. doi: 10.1542/peds.2013-2991.

Chapter Four

The Talent

It was hot in Los Angeles. Nothing unusual about that except it was December and only six days away from Christmas. In other cities around the U.S., a tickling of snow flurries symbolized the approach of a white Christmas. But that wasn't the case in the City of Angels. Blue skies with 100 percent chance of smog was the only thing in the forecast. The San Fernando Valley was no exception.

I journeyed north on the 405 toward the Valley, speeding down the freeway in unusually light traffic. A weird sense of anticipation grew as I approached America's hotbed for adult film production. In the U.S., only in the states of California and New Hampshire is it legal to produce hard-core porn. No other state legally allows it, likening pornography production to prostitution, making production in other locations a very risky and loosely enforced proposition.

As I exited, I expected to see huge billboards with scantily-clad women, or row after row of adult film studios. I didn't see any of that—just a regular city with regular people going about their daily lives, seemingly unaware that they worked and lived in the porn industry's epicenter.

What makes a person wake up one day and say, "I want to be a porn star"? Some say the pay is just too good to pass by, considering an actress can earn $1,000 a day for two hours of work. However, the money earned has no long-term residual effect—unlike the daughter of a friend of mine who played a tiny role in a major motion picture. Five years following the movie release date, her daughter continues to receive checks for the work performed. Adult films don't work that way. The pay that an actress earns for her work is not the gift that keeps on giving. There generally are no royalties.

Lack of royalty pay isn't the only item of concern. Because actors in adult films generally do not use condoms (unless they are covered by Los Angeles County's new condom law), the probability of contracting HIV and/or other STIs is a mathematical certainty without a complex and thorough health screening process. Sex workers submit to a battery of medical exams conducted on a regular basis, and their availability to work (or not) is tracked in a universal database accessible to producers.

Despite the images portrayed on camera, many adult film workers experience emotional turmoil due to their choice of profession and working conditions. Shelley Lubben's official website reveals some of the conditions workers in adult entertainment are exposed to:[1]

- "They told me if [I] had my AIDS test that I'd be safe. I arrived on the set with my test and did a hard-core scene with six men. Within that week I was very sick with a fever of 104 and blisters all over my mouth, throat, and private area. I looked like a monster. The doctor told me I had the non-curable disease genital herpes. I wanted to die." — Roxy, aka Shelley Lubben
- "After a year or so of that so-called 'glamorous' life, I sadly discovered that drugs and drinking were a part of the lifestyle. I began to drink and party out of control! Cocaine, alcohol, and ecstasy were my favorites. Before long, I turned into a person I did not want to be. After doing so many hard-core scenes, I couldn't do it anymore. I just remember being in horrible situations and experiencing extreme depression and being alone and sad." — Andi Anderson
- "I didn't want to feel the pain of penetration from an over-average-sized man; being told to freeze in a position until the cameraman was happy with his shots was very painful. I had people's body fluids forced on my face or anywhere else the producer pleased and I had to accept it or else no pay. Sometimes you would

get to a gig and the producer would change what the scene was supposed to be to something more intense, and again, if you didn't like it, too bad, you did it or no pay." — Elizabeth Rollings

- "The truth is I let my lifestyle get the best of me. I hate life. I'm a mess. A disaster. I've attempted suicide many times. No one cares about a dead porn star or stripper." — Neesa

Constance's Story

One night I was up at 2:30 in the morning, unable to sleep. I decided to get a jump-start on the day's work, so I booted up my trusty laptop. As I opened my e-mail, I was bombarded with ads offering everything from weight loss pills to pornography videos (it would seem that the wee hours of the morning is primetime for these types of ads). As I routinely began to delete the unwanted solicitations that always seemed to slip past my spam filter, an e-mail that read "Strip Church Las Vegas" caught my attention. Intrigued, I read further.

What drew my attention so early this particular morning was a four-minute, emotionally compelling short film posted on their website. The video characterized a thirteen-year-old girl named Constance who lives in the Philippines. Like most teenagers, Constance is consumed with her adolescent world of clothes, makeup, and music; however, what happens next is disturbing. Constance is temporarily sold and forced to have sex with an American man. This act is videotaped and later published on the Internet.

In the next scene, the short film depicts what happens when a likable guy with a young family (we'll call him Mr. Ordinary) views the sex act between Constance and the unidentified American man. Mr. Ordinary has a pornography secret that he's hiding from his family. And as he struggles in silence, he consumes the Internet images of thirteen-year-old Constance on his laptop right from the comfort of his living room table. He has no clue of the anguish and turmoil that Constance has endured since the making of that video. His insatiable appetite for porn seems to hamper his ability to distinguish between consensual sex versus statutory rape with an underage minor. After all, don't all participants in sexually explicit materials have to be eighteen years of age or older? Would Mr. Ordinary still watch this pornography if he knew that Constance's brothers sold her to a man that forced her to have sex with him?

The Constance video portrays a staggering reality about sexual images that are posted on some pornography websites. While the fantasy of porn may seem appealing, the atmosphere in which many adult films are created is chocked with pain, degradation, fear, exploitation, and even child abuse.

It could be that the porn you're watching is birthed from a woman's pain and suffering, not her sexual liberation. It could be that the porn you're watching is not consensual sex between two adults but instead represents a woman (or child) whose lifestyle has left her no other choice but to have sex on film in order to survive.

Think about the last sexually explicit material that you watched. What if you learned that the women having sex were not enjoying themselves at all but instead felt degraded and experienced great physical discomfort while making the video? What if you learned that these women were so financially strapped that they turned to porn as a desperate plan of last resort just to make a living? Would it affect your viewing habits? If you're viewing porn for entertainment, would it change your perception? ■

Endnotes

1. The website of Shelly Lubben, accessed December 30, 2014, https://www.shelleylubben.com/pornstars

Chapter Five

You, Me, and Your Porn Habit

On a typical weekday afternoon, my neighbor Debbie and I arrived home at the same time. As she slowly pulled into her driveway, the doors of her long SUV began to swing open. Three kids ranging in age from five to fifteen jumped from their seats, grabbing their backpacks and other belongings. As they all quickly exited, I heard a chorus of slamming doors, one after the other—bam, bam, bam, bam—as my neighbor's children walked up the porch and into the house.

I gave the obligatory wave and she waved back, but today was different. Debbie called out my name and moved toward my driveway. Despite my tight schedule, I met her halfway and we began to chat about our kids, school activities, the weather, and the crazy woman who lived two houses down the street. Our conversation comfortably shifted into a discussion about Debbie's husband.

"You know my husband; he's *always* out in the garage doing this and that. I can barely get him to come in the house to spend time with me," Debbie said.

"Really?" I said. "Well, you know how men are with their garages. Take the TV out of there and put the game on in the house—that should get him back inside." We both laughed, knowing how much of a sports nut her husband is. I could sense there was something more Debbie wanted to share with me.

"It's more than just the garage. Even when he's in the house he spends most of his time in his office with the door shut. It's like he's not really here with us, and the kids are starting to notice."

"That's strange," I mumbled. I began to wonder what *was* going on with her husband. He's a pleasant guy and a hard worker. Unlike the rest of us in the neighborhood who had outsourced our lives, he's the type of man that does his own work. He cuts his own grass, washes his own car, and cleans his own pool.

Debbie continued, "I've asked him what's wrong, but he always says everything's fine and changes the subject."

"Do you think he's stressed out about his job?"

"No, I don't think that's it," Debbie said as she shook her head. "He's got a new boss that he actually likes." Debbie moved the conversation back to her husband's behavior. "When he finally comes to bed, he doesn't make any moves on me and goes straight to sleep."

With that comment my eyes widened and immediately I stifled a whispered giggle, somewhat embarrassed as the conversation suddenly shifted to the intimate details of Debbie's sex life.

Was he cheating? I had known them both for over fifteen years, and her husband having an affair seemed far-fetched to me.

"I wonder what's going on with him?" I pondered out loud, attempting to shift the conversation back to safer pastures.

Debbie continued, "So I try to make the moves on him and he seems interested at first but then..." she hesitated, "that just doesn't work out." Debbie avoided my eyes and looked down at the ground. I could see the beginnings of sadness wash over her face.

"Deb, what do *you* think the problem is?" I asked her pointedly.

And then she shared the big shocker. She told me that she felt her husband was obsessed with pornography and that she was certain he was watching it on a regular basis. She told me that he didn't invite her to watch and that she was feeling excluded from his life. She blamed herself for his behavior and felt it was her responsibility to become more "sexy" in their bedroom to win back his affections.

What my neighbor described is not uncommon with married couples that are struggling with heavy porn consumption. When a person becomes hooked on sexually explicit materials, their desire to have sex with their spouse can become perfunctory or nonexistent.

Up until now we've discussed female pornography consumption; however, I'd like to present a different perspective—the emotional challenges women face when their spouse or significant other becomes hooked on pornography.

Pornography often portrays a fantasy world where anything goes and beautiful people have sex with no rules or consequences. Sex in public places or sex with a forbidden partner (a teacher, the boss, or someone else's spouse, for example) are all fair game. This can cause intimacy between a busy, married couple to pale in comparison, especially those who have fallen into a boring routine of sexual intercourse that lacks spark and excitement.

So what if you're a woman who suspects your husband or significant other is aggressively consuming porn? Have you noticed a change in your spouse's behavior? Is he distracted while you're having sex? Does he appear to be miles away rather than in the moment? Perhaps you've noticed he's not interested in being sexually intimate with you. Or has his sexual tastes and behaviors suddenly expanded beyond the ordinary and into a desire for kinky or aggressive sexual activities?

If you're in a relationship with someone who's struggling with a secret pornography compulsion, you're probably dealing with a variety of feelings and emotions. You've known for a while that something is different or wrong in your relationship. Because your significant other has been distant and/or unresponsive to your emotional needs, you may have developed feelings of doubt, insecurity, and/or low self-esteem. Perhaps you're a married woman who feels that your husband's viewing of sexually explicit material is directly related to your sexual expertise (or lack thereof). In response to your husband's waning affections, you now find yourself overcompensating by increasing the intensity of your lovemaking just to get his attention. Or perhaps you've done just the opposite. Maybe you have no desire to connect sexually with your spouse because you're suspicious of his secretive behavior.

Research conducted to study the effects of pornography consumption on romantic relationships found denial is one of the most common emotional responses a person might have when they learn that their significant other is watching pornography. If you suspect your husband is engaged with pornography, you may be ignoring the signs out of fear that your suspicions are confirmed. You may be overly concerned about what others will say and therefore take comfort in denying the truth.

It's painful to face the reality that your spouse enjoys pornography just as much or more than having sex with you. Learning of your husband's dependence on porn may stir up a wide range of emotions, everything from shock, anger, and resentment to a sense of failure and insecurity about your own sexuality. Whatever emotions you might be feeling, it's important not to ignore them.

*****

Let's look at porn consumption from a different perspective. What if you're the one in the relationship that's been secretly watching porn or reading erotica? If you achieve your sexual satisfaction from the screen of a computer or the pages of a book, subconsciously you may find yourself comparing your spouse to the characters you view or read about: *My husband doesn't have the same stamina like the men I see on the Internet. He needs to try harder.* Or, *My husband is not into B&D (bondage and domination); he's a sexual bore.* Your tolerance level for porn may be so high that you expect an unattainable sexual nirvana with every instance of lovemaking.

Sexual intimacy between a husband and wife can and should be a wonderful, exciting, invigorating, and enjoyable experience; however, continuous exposure to pornography creates a fantasy that is far from most people's everyday reality. In real life, couples have to work hard at maintaining their relationships. In real life people do have sexual boundaries and are not willing to perform every conceivable sexual fetish. In real life, emulating themes found in pornography, such as group sex and sex with other married couples, can cause you to lose your marriage. Sexually explicit material can undermine healthy monogamous relationships and negatively impact sexual intimacy.

Tug-of-War

Several years ago, my friend Bruce told me that he had been diagnosed with cancer. This came as a shock because Bruce is a young man, very much into fitness, and lives an overall healthy lifestyle. We discussed the diagnosis and treatment of his condition. He was amazingly optimistic.

"There's more to this cancer thing that I've got to tell you," Bruce said with a long sigh. "I haven't told anyone in my family that I've been diagnosed."

"What?" I exclaimed.

"I know," Bruce said as his voice trailed off.

"How long have you known?" There was a long pause on the other end of the phone line. Bruce chose his words carefully before he spoke.

"I've known for several months."

I couldn't believe it. Bruce comes from a large family and he's very close to his mother. In fact, we affectionately call him a "mama's boy." The fact that he hadn't told his siblings or his mom made no sense to me.

"Bruce," I pleaded, "why haven't you told anyone? We all love you very much. You don't have to go through this alone." I paused, searching for something more to say. "Your mother really doesn't know anything about this?"

"I can't tell my mother. She wouldn't take this well. All she'd do is worry herself sick. 'Did you eat? Did you go to the doctor? Did you get enough rest?'" Bruce mimicked his mom's voice.

Bruce exhaled heavily and continued, "It's hard enough for me to wrap my mind around what's happening—the changes I feel in my body. I'm weak all the time and I don't have the energy to do the things I like to do. If my mother knew this, it would be too much for her."

"Oh my gosh, Bruce," I muttered.

"I need all of my strength to beat this," he said. "I just don't have the energy to make it okay for me *and* for Mom."

While I don't know if I'd take the same approach as Bruce, I did understand the rationale. It's the same struggle your spouse or significant other may have with fighting a pornography habit. Let's say that you've just learned your spouse is hooked on porn. In hindsight you noticed signs that hinted at the problem, such as frequent viruses on the computer, unexplained charges on the debit card bill, or initiation of unusual or kinky sex.

If your spouse has hidden his struggle from you, it could be that the combination of resisting porn and helping you cope with his addiction are too overwhelming for him. Just as my friend Bruce felt strong and optimistic about fighting the cancer, his strength turned to despair at the thought of having to make it "okay" for his mom. He felt he couldn't be successful in the battle if his energy was spent on encouraging his mother through his illness. Your spouse may also feel that kicking a pornography habit will be more difficult with your involvement, particularly if he believes you will not be supportive or sympathetic.

What can you do to help? If your spouse or significant other is struggling with heavy porn consumption, ask him to identify those things and/or situations that trigger a desire to watch pornography. Then, take an inventory of your home to remove as much temptation as you can. Seemingly harmless items such as lingerie magazine advertisements or unmonitored Internet access can trigger a porn relapse. Also, encourage your spouse to get an accountability partner and don't be offended if you're not offered the role. The truth is, you may not be the best choice.

So yes, maybe you've been hurt by your husband's lies. Or maybe you've lost all faith in your significant other because of broken promises to stop watching porn. Your feelings of betrayal are real and should not be discounted; but remember that your loved one may be right in the middle of the tug-of-war of a lifetime, stretched to the max by an insatiable desire for pornography and a desperate struggle to kick the habit.

The road to victory over pornography is often a zigzag, not a straight line. Don't let a setback spoil the comeback! View every positive step your spouse makes, no matter how small, as a step in the right direction to become porn-free. And finally, if you're a woman who's heavily consuming porn, I pray that this chapter has helped you see how your actions may impact your spouse or significant other, and I encourage you to make a genuine commitment to eliminating pornography from your life.

In Chapter 7 I will share specifics steps you can take to not only break a pornography habit, but to maintain abstinence going forward. However, before we get there, let's take a closer look at the warning signs that indicate when pornography consumption has moved beyond casual. ■

Chapter Six

Looked or Hooked?

Jessica, a busy stay-at-home mom, was going out with the girls. She didn't get out very often, so she was particularly intrigued when her good friend coyly mentioned, "I've got something really special for you guys that you're going to love!"

As Jessica drove to her friend's home, she wondered what surprise she would encounter. Was it a new bottle of wine? Or perhaps a big announcement that one of her friends was getting married or having a baby? All this speculation fueled Jessica's excitement for the evening.

Upon arrival, Jessica began to hug and kiss the party guests, women she had known for many years. Many were old friends from junior high school, and all were established women actively engaged in thriving careers. And this wasn't a bachelorette party; the married women outnumbered the singles two to one.

Jessica hadn't been there long when she discovered the surprise the hostess had mentioned. This was no ordinary GNO. The evening gathering was to be a product party. But instead of Tupperware or jewelry, the items on sale were erotic toys. As the party got under way, the host described every item that was for sale. Jessica had never seen any of these items before, but her curiosity was piqued. Although there was much schoolgirl giggling, there were periods of complete silence as the women watched in amazement.

After the formal presentation, Jessica closely browsed the items on display. She felt embarrassed by the idea of bringing anything from the table home to her husband; however, she ultimately decided to purchase a simple vibrator.

Months later, Jessica and I spoke on the phone.

"It's my eleven o'clock appointment," Jessica said, ready to cut the call short.

"What do you mean eleven o'clock appointment?" I replied, matching Jessica's matter-of-fact tone.

"There's always so much goin' on in my house. After the kids are gone and Mike's on the road, I do a few things around the house, run errands, and then I'm back home around eleven o'clock. That's when I pull out old faithful."

I paused for a moment, trying to follow what Jessica was telling me. "Okay, you lost me. What is it that you're doing at 11:00?" I asked point-blank.

"You know..." Jessica hesitated, "the little toy I bought at Terri's party."

"Uh," I said, still trying to put it together. Then suddenly the realization hit. "Ohhhh, *that* party!"

"Yes, yes."

I grew silent. Jessica and I typically didn't discuss intimate details like this, so I wasn't sure where the conversation was heading.

Jessica continued, "I've become addicted to this thing. I use it every day. Yesterday I found myself in the kids' room taking batteries out of their toys."

"Oh... wow," I said as I began to chuckle. I knew Jessica was revealing something very important to me, but I couldn't help but see humor in her stealing batteries from her kids' video game controller. Jessica went on to tell me that she began to watch pornography while using the vibrator. Just like coffee with cream, she no longer could have one without the other.

*****

I've heard the term "epidemic" used to describe our society's consumption of pornographic materials. Despite this growing trend, there's limited academic and scientific data on this topic and its effect on the individual, family, and society. Researchers struggle with how to measure and evaluate pornography use because traditional surveys fall short as participants under-report how much they're truly using porn. There are few tools to help prevent or resolve pornography compulsions. One trip to a large bookstore chain will reveal an impressive display of self-help books ranging from personal money management to emotional well-being and spiritual renewal—but there is very little on dealing with pornography.

Porn is the secret that many people are engaged in but few will admit to. While scrolling my Facebook newsfeed, I came across a status update from a woman that read "I like porn!" Curious to read the comments to this bold statement, I quickly clicked the post and to my surprise, there were absolutely no comments. No "me too," no "TMI," not even a single "like" to acknowledge her proclamation. Just digital silence. I suspect this woman is not the only person in her Facebook network that watches porn, but no one else was willing to publically admit their consumption or agree with her statement.

When chatting with an old friend during a lunch event, she showed me a collection of pornographic images maintained on her smartphone. In her possession she had soft-core animated porn and also an image of a male penis that had been casually texted to her. The showstopper included a hard-core bestiality photo that she had no problem sharing openly.

I inquired further and immediately saw a pattern beginning to develop. What started with a seemingly harmless sexually suggestive cartoon had morphed into progressively raunchy photos. I could sense that this young woman had viewed (and showed) those pictures so many times that she had become desensitized to their impact.

I have no idea at what level (if any) this woman uses pornography today, but it's important to understand that even indiscriminate viewing can lead to an increased desire to view more explicit images to satisfy a growing level of porn tolerance. It reminds me of my friend Sharon who doesn't like to take painkillers at the first sign of illness. When I asked her why, she told me she's concerned that her body will adjust to the drug and the medicine will lose its ability to deliver relief. She feels that it's too easy to build up a tolerance, therefore dictating the need for more pills (or a stronger dose) to eliminate the same level of discomfort.

While there are certainly recreational porn users who may never have a desire to go beyond casual consumption, I fear many more start off as occasional viewers and quickly build up a tolerance that propels them to seek more hard-core videos or emulate in real life what they've been watching over and over. Like Sharon's pain pill concern, can casual pornography consumption be a precursor to building a tolerance to sexually explicit materials?

Initial exposure to pornography often elicits a variety of emotions ranging from shock and disgust to curiosity and excitement. When viewing a sexually explicit video, you may find it so arousing that you decide to watch again. If you are like many who couple masturbation and pornography together, you may find that repeated exposure to the same material causes the thrill to eventually fade. A common response, therefore, is to watch more porn for longer periods of time, or graduate to hard-core images to duplicate the original sensation. Achieving the same high often requires more graphic sexually explicit images. Therapists refer to this as *tolerance*.

If you've experienced this progression, this may signal that your pornography viewing has shifted beyond casual entertainment to compulsive behavior. Remember, there's no specific profile of an excessive pornography user. Habitual consumption can affect men and women, youth and adults. Your economic, marital, and/or educational status is all irrelevant.

Researchers and therapists debate the characterization of excessive pornography consumption as addiction. The American Society of Addiction Medicine defines *addiction* as:

> "[The] inability to consistently abstain, impairment in behavioral control, craving, diminished recognition

of significant problems with one's behaviors and interpersonal relationships, and a dysfunctional emotional response. Like other chronic diseases, addiction often involves cycles of relapse and remission."

I experienced some of these reactions. For me, it was hard to abstain from watching porn even when I wanted to. I recall a time when I was so conflicted by what I was viewing in relation to my faith and spiritual beliefs that in one impulsive moment I threw away my entire hidden porn stash. And I didn't just toss it into the kitchen trash. No, I dumped it all in the outside garbage container and watched the trash truck haul it away. But because I had not made a genuine commitment to stop consuming porn and because I had not confessed my struggle to anyone else to help stay accountable to abstinence, shortly after I fell back into the same cycle as I slowly repurchased a new stock of sexually explicit materials.

So where do you fall when it comes to viewing pornography? Have your tastes expanded over time, demanding more explicit material? Do you find it difficult to resist the temptation to read erotica? Do you find yourself preoccupied with thoughts of pornography? Maybe you're frequently thinking about the images that you've viewed or the sex acts you've seen in an adult film. Perhaps you're so consumed with viewing porn or reading erotic stories that it negatively impacts how you feel and respond to your partner. Or do you find yourself masturbating to pornography in lieu of cultivating a healthy, sustainable relationship with your spouse? Have you attempted to emulate the sexual activities you read about? Have you stopped consuming porn altogether, only to fall right back into it? Have you looked, or are you hooked?

When we develop a pattern of watching pornography, we're exposed to unrealistic images of sexual intercourse, as well as themes that promote infidelity and sex outside of marriage. These images, viewed frequently, can become more familiar and acceptable, whether you believe pornography is good, bad, right, or wrong.

Consider the following: There's a popular fast-food burger restaurant in my city. The menu is pretty simple and consists of burgers, fries, and drinks. Day or night, you can count on a long line of cars snaking throughout the parking lot anxiously awaiting their burgers. To attract customers, the advertising gurus created the ultimate billboard—a thirty-foot high display of a huge cheeseburger that towers over several heavily travelled freeways. The burger "oozes" with all the fixin's as steam wafts out, giving the appearance that it's hot and fresh off the grill. On many occasions I've seen that sign and pulled over to grab a burger, which I'm sure is exactly what the marketing execs had in mind. This company understands how people are influenced and motivated by what they see.

Why would this company or any corporation spend thousands and even millions of dollars to market their products and services if consumers weren't influenced by what they see? The goal is to put a product or service right before our eyes on a repeated basis to stir up the desire to buy. Feed the people an image over and over until the people identify the brand and desire the product or service. Whether its food, electronics, or fashion, if the image is shown on a repeated and continuous basis, it will generate a demand and desire for that product.

Pornography is no different. When you view it regularly, it's easy to become influenced by its themes and images that de-emphasize love, commitment, and marriage. When your consumption becomes part of your lifestyle, you've greatly increased your likelihood of acting on the images you see (or the text you read).

For example, the popular book *Fifty Shades of Grey* has reportedly influenced the sexual behavior of its wide fan base. Handcuff mishaps, for those new to the book's B&D genre, and increased sales of the book's sex toys are just a couple of the behaviors women are emulating all across the country. However, for some, the activities they ingest from *Shades* are not as harmless. In a study conducted by Michigan State University, researchers found some correlation between young adult women who read the book and their likelihood of engaging with a verbally abusive partner much like the lead character in the *Fifty Shades* saga.[1]

Continuously watching sexually explicit material can influence your sexual beliefs, appetites, and behaviors. Over time, it's possible you'll emulate what you frequently see; if you're agreeable to what's seen, you can easily copycat the actions and behaviors portrayed in sexually explicit materials. In a study of close to 1,000 sex addicts, 90 percent of the men and 77 percent of the women interviewed reported pornography consumption as a significant contributor toward their sexual addictions.[2] We're talking about people who, because of watching pornography, have gotten addicted to sex at such dangerous levels that they've sought clinical assistance for their problem.

There's a serious risk of allowing strong sexual content to become part of your everyday life. In many films, characters do not practice safe sex—nor do they contract AIDS, STDs, or get pregnant. Casual and indiscriminate sex generally has no consequences in such portrayals—a huge misconception that porn consumers ingest.

*****

Pornography can be extremely habit-forming and can quickly desensitize you to the images that you view. One can easily become accepting of sexual intercourse between unmarried men and women, sexual intercourse between taboo partners or strangers, sexual intercourse without the use of protection, and sexual intercourse between multiple partners (group sex). If you ingest an image over and over again, burning it into your mind and spirit, it can become more familiar to you. The more familiar these behaviors become, the more likely you are to emulate them over time. Familiarity breeds emulation.

In the next chapter I'm going to show you how to take a spiritual cleanse and implement effective strategies to help break a pornography habit. ■

Endnotes

1. Bonomi Amy E., Nemeth Julianna M., Altenburger Lauren E., Anderson Melissa L., Snyder Anastasia, and Dotto Irma, *Journal of Women's Health,* September 2014, 23(9). doi:10.1089/jwh.2014.4782.

2. Patrick J. Carnes, *Don't Call it Love,* New York: Bantam Books, 2013.

Chapter Seven

Spiritual Cleanse

Over a period of about two years, I gained weight by making unhealthy food choices. To me, a relaxing Friday night meant baking and eating almost an entire batch of brownies with ice cold milk. I fell into a phase where I was eating all the wrong things, mostly fast food. Just as kryptonite makes Superman weak, French fries had the same effect on my resolve to eat healthy. Over time, my eating habits robbed me of energy and made me lethargic. Eventually I had to buy new clothes because I could no longer fit my old outfits. I wanted to lose weight and get fit, but my desire to change didn't overpower my appetite for junk food. I tried easy fixes like dieter's tea and colon cleanses, but I continuously found myself in the same rut.

Many people go through this same dilemma when trying to kick their pornography habit. It could be that watching porn leaves you feeling guilty, but no matter how intense those feelings are, it doesn't override your desire to watch more explicit material. You may have a desire to ditch the habit, but you just don't have the willpower to remain committed to your plan. You may feel hopeless because every time you try to quit, within a short matter of months, weeks, or even days, you start back up again.

One day I got on the scale and became completely frustrated with what I saw and decided I was going to make life changes in my health, eating, and fitness. So I did some research and got on an eating plan and started exercising. Three months later, I had lost twenty-five pounds and was going strong. I was two dress sizes slimmer, had lots of energy, and felt very satisfied with my results.

One secret to my success was that I chose an eating plan that was forgiving. If I fell off the wagon with my diet, this plan taught me how to redirect, get up, and keep going. I was forbidden to feel guilty or come down hard on myself for consuming unhealthy foods. I needed this because there were lots of slips along the way. I was encouraged to remain positive despite any setback, no matter how small or large.

Another reason that I was successful at losing weight was that I solicited the help of others for encouragement. I joined an online community with other people who were on the same plan as I was and we all held each other accountable. I attended workout classes at the gym and developed friendships with others who shared my same passion for fitness and nutrition. We encouraged each other to stay fit and made the right food choices.

Even though my weight loss came rather quickly, it was not without hard work and great discipline. I remember wanting desperately to lose pounds but feeling so hopeless because I couldn't stop myself from eating the junk food I craved so much. I didn't have the self-control to do it on my own. I'd eat healthy for a little while, then I'd stop. Eat healthy, eat junk food. Back and forth and back and forth. But when I shared my goals with people who wanted to see me succeed, and when I created associations with others who were involved in the same fitness activities that I was, I began to see real progress, real quick.

These same weight-loss principles can be applicable when kicking a pornography compulsion, and they include:

- Making a true commitment to quit consuming sexually explicit materials
- Forgiving yourself if you have a setback (or setbacks)
- Connecting with at least one other person to take your porn secret out of the closet to help you remain accountable
- Exercising the required discipline to retain your abstinence

Detoxification Protocol

We live in an age that emphasizes the importance of healthy living. These days, we can walk into a fast-food restaurant and find grilled chicken instead of cheeseburgers, or fresh fruit instead of French fries. What we ingest directly impacts our body, mind, and soul. Years of poor eating can hinder our ability to operate at an optimal level. Just ask the lucrative cold-press juicing industry whose signature mantra is detoxification. They understand the importance of removing toxins from the body and replacing them with nutritious elixirs.

We can take this same approach in fighting the temptation to view pornography. To receive sustainable results in this area, we first need to detox the images of, and desire for, sexually explicit material. Don't worry—there are no green juices to muscle down. This is our spiritual cleanse.

Detoxification Protocol

Confess

Commit

Account

Detoxing is a three-step process that begins when you confess your struggle with pornographic materials to yourself and one other person. Confession is an essential step to release feelings of shame, guilt, and isolation. Confessing my struggles to a friend—and because of my spiritual beliefs to God as well—was a turning point for me. It released the burden of carrying my porn secret. The act of acknowledging your struggle to someone else will bolster your resolve to abstain. Confession is a foundational step in the detox process and should not be skipped.

The second step in the detox process requires that you commit, genuinely, to stop watching porn. Up until now, you may not have made a true decision to quit. It's hard to do, I know. When I was struggling with watching porn, I told myself many times that I would stop; however, my words were hollow statements, void of any real power, because my heart did not match my thoughts. Sometimes we need to *build* up the desire to *have* the desire. Make an honest commitment to yourself and at least one other person to quit, and if you are a person of faith, make that vow to God as well. An authentic pledge to yourself, another person, and to God, if you so choose, will help kick-start your discipline to abstain.

Make the commitment TODAY to stop consuming. Record this day in your journal or in your planner to mark the significance of this decision. Even if you think you might break the commitment, make it anyway. Your ability to abstain from pornography with one bold decision is not the measurement of success, but that bold decision to quit can be the catalyst that gets the ball rolling.

The final step in the detox process requires that you account yourself to another person as you learn to abstain from porn. Covenant Eyes, makers of Internet filtering software, defines accountability as the willingness to give an account to someone else of your actions and motives. Confiding to another person or participating in a support group/program that promotes abstinence will help to remove the power that your porn secret has over your life. Here are some strategies you can implement today to develop accountability:

- Reach out to someone you trust and confess your challenge to them privately. Ask that person to support you as an accountability partner in your journey toward abstinence.
- Join a support group or online forum that assists women who are attracted to pornography or erotica. (Please see the appendix for a resource list.) Allow yourself to genuinely connect with others who share your struggle.
- Based on your level of need, consider joining a formal recovery program geared specifically for women who are challenged with pornography or erotica consumption. Don't worry about who will know. These are

confidential programs that will respect your privacy, and some are web-based. I've listed several reputable resources in the appendix such as X3Pure. This program is geared toward women struggling with behaviors that have become compulsive, including pornography use, masturbation, and extra-marital/pre-marital sex.

If you prefer to develop a relationship with an accountability partner, schedule regular check-ins on a weekly, bi-weekly, or monthly basis (in the beginning, you may need more frequent interaction). Your check-ins can be as informal as text or e-mail messages, or more structured with phone calls or face-to-face meetings. Phone calls worked best for me.

During your accountability check-in, you'll want to share your successes and share your plans for correction if you've experienced any setbacks. You'll also want to contact your partner immediately when you're feeling tempted. The role of your accountability partner is not only to lend an encouraging ear as you walk this journey, but to ask the tough questions about your porn consumption when you're evasive or unreachable.

To hold you accountable, your partner does not have to be someone who has struggled with porn, but if they have, ensure they have a solid track record of abstinence (usually at least one year). For me, I've had two accountability partners, one who did struggle with porn, and one who had not. Both women had two different approaches and styles. The one who had never struggled with porn was less sympathetic, particularly when I was making excuses for my behavior, and instead offered a "tough love" approach. I needed this when my setbacks became too frequent. Alternatively, the other woman who had experienced the same issues that I had was more comforting. While she didn't condone my slipups, she could relate to them and that was helpful. For me, I benefited greatly from partnering with both of these women at different periods of time.

Some of you may feel so overwhelmed with protecting your porn secret that you commit to stop watching with no accountability from another person, process, or program. Going it alone is the hardest way to get results because it's easy for you to slip back into watching porn with no one to hold you accountable. Don't keep your struggle a secret. Don't let private thoughts of embarrassment, shame, and humiliation prevent you from seeking help from a trustworthy person or source. Sharing your challenges with another person in a safe environment, whether online, via phone/text, or in person, is one of the best ways to ensure your success.

This process of detoxification, which includes confessing, committing, and becoming accountable, is essential to overcoming pornography attractions. In addition, you will need to ***monitor*** your triggers. Your triggers are the people, places, situations, and/or emotions that stir up a desire in you to view or read sexually explicit material. In our highly sexualized culture, many things we are exposed to can trigger the desire to connect with pornography. Maybe it's the TV show that you watch or the music that you listen to. Or maybe certain times of the day or night have become your triggers. A glass of wine late at night might put you in the mood to watch porn or read erotica. Fights with your spouse or significant other might also be a trigger. Loneliness is a dangerous culprit that can easily lead to an increased desire to connect with explicit content. Learn to resist the urge to view pornography by monitoring your triggers.

As you begin to implement these steps, prepare to experience a stronger than normal desire to start watching or reading again. If this happens, don't become discouraged or give up. Often the final lap of a race is the most challenging and requires the most intensive output of endurance and strength. If you stumble, firmly re-establish the detoxification protocols of confession, commitment, and accountability in your life, identify the circumstance(s) that led to the setback, make the appropriate adjustment to prevent future challenges, and most importantly, keep moving forward.

I once read a fitness book where the author implored the reader not to give up the pursuit of weight loss just because of weight gain, particularly on a week when you've done everything according to plan. He said the road to success is rarely straight and often curves from left to right. Every week provides an opportunity to collect and record data. If you gain weight, reflect back on what you ate and how you exercised (or lack thereof). Analyze the data, make adjustments, and continue moving forward to achieve the goal. Likewise, any time you fall short of your abstinence goal, reflect on what you can do differently (did you monitor your triggers closely?) and make the adjustment. This isn't the time to give in.

Resisting temptation to watch porn will require great self-control. If you've ever lost weight after diligently managing your diet and exercise, you must remain committed to living a healthy lifestyle to retain your results. If you've straightened your teeth with braces, you must commit to wear the retainer. Keeping yourself free of the desire to view or read pornographic material is no different. Following the detoxification protocols and monitoring your triggers are essential. The rewards of abstinence are worth the hard work. One benefit for me is that I've been able to write this book to help those who have had the same challenges I've had.

Don't let one instance of weakness (or two or three) discourage you. While I'm sure there are some people who have stopped watching porn "cold turkey," for me it was a process of stopping and starting. Simply re-establish the detoxification protocols and continue to monitor your triggers. Stay fully committed to your porn abstinence, regardless of how things may appear on the outside, even if you've slipped up and watched again. Don't give up! You'll have successes and failures, but don't throw in the towel. Soon you will stop watching porn for longer periods of time until you're able to abstain altogether. ■

A Personal Note to You and an Introduction to the Concluding Chapters of this Book

The tools and techniques presented up to this point will assist you in stepping free of whatever hold pornography may have on you. They have proven effective for me and countless people—men and women—who have successfully walked away and stayed away from being involved with porn.

So, if you think you've gotten what you needed, it's fine for you to stop reading with this note.

However, the ideas presented in these last two chapters are ones that deepened my commitment to abstain and, for me, made it virtually certain that I would stay free.

What I cover from here on out are spiritual/scriptural in nature and have become part of my life and abiding faith. While the concepts are very real and personal for me, I recognize that others may not resonate with them. That's why I have included this as a bonus section. I wouldn't want anyone to negate the value of the previous chapters simply because of my personal spiritual beliefs.

For those open to the message of Scripture, I believe you will find added inspiration in these chapters. For those who aren't sure about them, I invite you to read on and explore whether they can open some doors inside of you for a greater sense of who we all are and what we are about.

Chapter Eight

Impure Spirits

Earlier in the book, we discussed how to break the spell pornography may have over your life. Specifically, we talked about detoxing the desires that are fueling your temptation to view more porn. I'd like to explore those urges further with a spiritual backdrop.

There's a supernatural battle occurring all around you, even as you read the pages of this book. It's a war between good and evil. Light and dark. Heaven and hell. This is an invisible fight that you cannot see, but you can feel. Scriptures tell us:

> "We are not fighting against humans. We are fighting against forces and authorities and against rulers of darkness and powers in the spiritual world." (Ephesians 6:12; Contemporary English Version)

Since before the beginning of time, Satan has always desired to disregard God's perfect plan for creation and exult himself above God's heavenly throne. However, his bid for dominance was unsuccessful and he was subsequently defeated (Isaiah 14:13–15). Despite this loss, he tries to outwit us with his schemes (2 Corinthians 2:11) through the use of spirits.

There are different kinds of spirits: those that are for your good, and those that are not (1 John 4:1). Bad spirits (sometimes referred to as "unclean" or "impure") are often employed by Satan with the ultimate goal of disrupting our fellowship with God. Consider the following Bible story of a man who was attacked by an impure spirit. He was in such bondage to it that he was forced into solitude, separated from his family. When Jesus encountered the man, the impure spirit within him responded:

> "What do you want with me, Jesus, Son of the Most High God? In God's name don't torture me!" (Mark 5:7; New International Version)

The impure spirit that had been warring inside the afflicted man was frightened. Jesus responded:

> "Come out of this man, you impure spirit!" (Mark 5:8; NIV)

Notice that Jesus didn't criticize or place blame on the tormented man for the condition that he was in; it was the impure spirit He was after. Subject to Christ's authority, the impure spirit was commanded to leave. Once free from its presence, the man regained control of his mind and body, profusely thanking Jesus for saving his life. Jesus told the man to return to his family and share with others this great news.

Any one of us can be vexed by impure spirits. While they will not cause your head to spin around in circles, nor will you spew green vomit, they can influence our actions by generating thoughts of lust, fornication, and adultery. The apostle Paul said it best:

> "I do not understand what I do. For what I want to do I do not do, but what I hate I do. As it is, it is no longer I myself who do it, but it is sin living in me. For I do not do the good I want to do, but the evil I do not want to do—this I keep on doing." (Romans 7:15–19; NIV)

Satan is like a ravenous lion roaming around looking for those he can devour (1 Peter 5:5). He and his crew of impure spirits are looking to gain entry into our lives. The Bible warns us that when we sin, it's possible to give him a foothold through our spiritual door (Ephesians 4:27). Sin can be overt like cheating, stealing, and lying, but it can also be covert. Review the list on the next page and ask yourself if you're struggling with any of these subtle sins that often lead to ungodly behavior:

- Limited or no communication with God through prayer
- Limited or no reading of Scripture
- Lack of self-control and discipline, especially toward those things that look good but aren't good for you
- Busyness and/or overextension of time and resources
- Idolatry of material things, activities, and/or loved ones
- Unforgiveness

Have you unintentionally allowed impure spirits to enter your spiritual house due to your ongoing refusal to forgive a friend or family member? Do you lack discipline in your life with limited ability to control excessive eating or shopping? Maybe you're not spending enough time with God through prayer and reading of Scripture, which has made you more susceptible to sexual sin?

This was an area that affected me. I was hit-and-miss with my Bible reading at best, satisfied to be fed a great sermon on Sunday. I lacked the desire and discipline to pray and study God's Word on my own, not realizing how important this was toward evicting impure spirits and stopping my porn attraction. If you're consuming pornography despite your best efforts to quit, it's possible that you cannot resist due to the influence of impure spirits brought on by continuous, remorseless sin in your life.

Jesus gave all twelve of the disciples the power to cast out impure spirits. This was the first authority He provided, even before the ability to heal sickness and disease (Matthew 10:1). The Savior knew the disciples would need to cast out these spirits on a regular basis and this need still exists today.

In our modern churches, we rarely mention impure or evil spirits as if Satan is no longer in the evil-doing business. However, impure spirits are very much a part of the world we live in. If we're not aware of them or if we don't study the Bible to learn how to defeat and avoid them, we can find ourselves subject to them.

Say the following prayer to ask God to remove impure spirits from your life:

All things are possible through You, Lord, even overcoming the most difficult challenges. I know there is nothing that I cannot accomplish when I am connected to You. I can do all things through Christ who strengthens me. I know the purposes that You have for me are good, plans to prosper me in a variety of ways. I take comfort in knowing that Your purposes will not be thwarted, even if my current situation looks irredeemable. Search my heart, oh Lord, and know that I desire to break the hold that pornography has over my life. I pray this day that You will remove any impure spirits that may be influencing my desire to consume porn. Today I make a genuine commitment to abstain from pornography. I know, at times, it may be difficult to stand firm in this commitment; however, let me choose righteousness over lasciviousness, let me choose life in the spirit over death in the flesh, let me choose You over porn. I thank You in advance for an overflow of Your grace. I know it is sufficient to help me stay committed to abstinence. In Jesus' name I pray, amen.

Don't let the Deceiver trick you into thinking this simple prayer will not work for your situation or complex problem. Seeking God in your greatest time of need is supposed to be uncomplicated. In fact, Scripture tells us:

> "Come to me, all you who are weary and burdened, and I will give you rest. Take my yoke upon you and learn from me, for I am gentle and humble in heart, and you will find rest for your souls. For my yoke is easy and my burden is light." (Matthew 11:28–30; NIV)

In addition to petitioning God to remove impure spirits from your life, you must implement the detoxification protocol that we discussed in Chapter 7 to strengthen your resolve to abstain from pornography. Remember to ***confess*** your struggle to God and at least one other person; make an authentic ***commitment*** to stop watching porn; become ***accountable*** to another person; and ***monitor*** your triggers. Once you take these steps, you'll be well on your way to eliminating the control that pornography has over your life.

*****

I remember the morning I made the commitment to stop watching porn. I was at church and a guest minister was speaking about the spiritual consequences of sexual sin. I had never heard this subject discussed so openly at a Sunday morning service. Frozen in my seat, I stared straight ahead, too afraid to look to the left or right in fear that someone might guess my porn secret. And this was at a time when pornography attraction was a problem reserved exclusively for men.

God spoke to me that day through the courageous message of that minister. At the close of service, I made a genuine decision to stop watching porn as I boldly stood up out of my seat and made my way to the altar at the front of the church. Could I have made this commitment while seated in the pew or sitting at home in my living room? Absolutely, but for me, going to the altar was an important and symbolic gesture; it was an outward demonstration of my inward resolve to do my part to abstain.

You will need help from God and others to break the influence pornography has over your life. Remember the afflicted man in the Bible story? He also needed help. He was so unhappy with his existence that he began to physically cut himself (Mark 5:5). To prevent the man from causing greater harm, he was restrained:

> "Whenever he was put into chains and shackles—as he often was—he snapped the chains from his wrists and smashed the shackles." (Mark 5:4; New Living Translation)

The restraints that were placed on this man were put there for his own protection; however, he continuously broke them. I see this as a powerful metaphor. By smashing his own restraints, he was in essence rejecting the help that others attempted to offer him.

When I was struggling with pornography, I suffered in silence out of fear of what others, particularly my church friends, might think of me. Without realizing it, I rejected those who might have helped me. Because I allowed my guilt to consume me, I didn't confide in anyone—and I missed opportunities to receive support and encouragement.

Abstaining from pornography will require that you seek God's help just as the afflicted man did. When he first saw Jesus in the distance, he came running out to meet Him. I want you to catch this. Even though Jesus was still far away, the man *ran* toward Him and fell to his knees at Jesus' feet (Mark 5:6; NIV). He didn't *wait* for the Savior to come to him, rather he went to the Savior as fast as he could.

Trying to kick a porn habit on your own without God's help will put you at a significant disadvantage. It reminds me of Christians who have walked away from God, saying, "I have to get my life together first, then I'll come back to church." In reality, they need God to get their life together, not the other way around. You are not the only woman struggling with porn, or any habitual sin, for that matter. Even the famous figures of the Bible were challenged with making the right choices in life. In Romans 7:24–25, the apostle Paul says of himself:

> "Oh, what a miserable person I am! Who will free me from this life that is dominated by sin and death? Thank God! The answer is in Jesus Christ our Lord." (NLT)

No one is perfect, but Paul reminds us that there is a solution to every problem we face. When we put God first, we receive the willpower and discipline we need to abstain from pornography.

*****

Once the impure spirits have split, and the temptation and desire to view pornography has begun to subside, you must prevent the spirits from returning by refilling your spiritual house. Scriptures tell us:

> "When an impure spirit comes out of a person, it goes through arid places seeking rest and does not find it.

> Then it says, 'I will return to the house I left.' When it arrives, it finds the house unoccupied, swept clean and put in order. Then it goes and takes with it seven other spirits more wicked than itself, and they go in and live there. And the final condition of that person is worse than the first." (Matthew 12:43–45; NIV)

Notice that when the impure spirit returned, it found the house (the person) cleaned out and empty. Although previously detoxified, there was nothing to block the spirit's return. When no measures are taken to prevent infestation by impure spirits, they can return with more force and destruction than before. Our spiritual home must be swept clean *and* refilled.

Let me present this concept in a more practical illustration. Each year Southern California has a wildfire season. The winds are high, the terrain is dry, and the temperatures are hot. A small fire easily contained during other times of the year can quickly grow out of control to become destructive and life-threatening.

One season, the region was struck hard. Multiple fires burned simultaneously, quickly charring thousands of acres, killing animals, and destroying homes; however, one particular community experienced no loss of property. This neighborhood had been ravaged by wildfires before, but it had been strategically rebuilt to prevent future fire devastation.

The first time this neighborhood was impacted by wildfires, there was great destruction and loss of property. Naturally, the immediate response was to contain and extinguish the fire. Next, a commitment was made to rebuild this community in a manner that would reduce the likelihood of future damage. To accomplish this, new homes were constructed with tiled roofs as opposed to flammable wood shingles. Large bushes and trees were planted an appropriate distance away to prevent the quick spread of fire from foliage to structure. A wide green belt containing fire-resistant bushes and an extensive sprinkler system was planted around the perimeter of the housing tract for additional protection.

Notice the pattern of detoxification and refilling. In order to re-establish the new community, the burnt out mess of the first fire had to be removed. To prevent future devastation, it wasn't enough to just rebuild new homes. Instead, preventive measures such as tiled roofs and the fire-resistant green belt were put in place. If these defensive tactics had not been implemented, the community could have suffered the same destruction it had experienced years ago, possibly worse.

Once you've asked God to remove impure spirits and you've implemented the three-step detoxification protocol, refilling of your spiritual house must begin. You can do this by developing a regular prayer life, connecting with the Word of God, and monitoring your triggers. Prayer, at its core, is having a conversation with God. To ***pray*** regularly means that you speak with God on a consistent basis. I prefer to pray first thing in the morning before I start my day. The stillness of early morning and the clarity of thought at this time is ideal for me.

You may find it hard to pray if you're not in the habit of praying regularly. Here's a simple format that I have practiced for years and have had great success with. I begin by praising God. The Bible describes God in a multitude of ways, such as being loving (John 3:16), holy (Isaiah 6:3), powerful (1 Chronicles 29:11), merciful (Hebrews 4:16), and the list goes on and on. I simply repeat these accolades back to God. Then I begin to thank God for all that He has done for me. I always remember to thank God for things we often take for granted, such as being alive, the use of all my limbs and faculties, and having a comfortable home to live in. Next I confess my sins, the stuff I've done intentionally and unintentionally (such as putting other priorities before God).

Skeptics may feel that seeking forgiveness is pointless since no one is perfect and we ultimately will sin again. I disagree. I think God is looking at our hearts, not at how successful we are (or are not). When we pray and express a genuine desire to change bad behavior, God sees this and He appreciates it. Our environment begins to shift ever so slightly as He moves things in our favor to help us make better choices and become all that He's called us to be. And finally, I ensure that I pray for others such as my family, friends, co-workers, and even people that I don't know. After I have completed these items, I speak to God about whatever is on my heart, including requests for help or a confession of a challenge.

In addition to regular prayer, it is essential to ***connect*** with God's Word by reading the Bible on a regular basis to refill your spiritual house. One system that really helped me was to read Scriptures from a Bible app on my tablet, such as youversion.com. The iPad's super-convenient, always "on" technology has effectively eliminated the old excuses I had for not reading the Bible. (If you're not sure how to effectively study Scriptures, try reading pastor Rick Warren's *Bible Study Methods*. It's an excellent guide.)

Even when you don't feel tempted to fall back into pornography, continue to read and reflect on Scriptures regularly. As you do this, God will birth new dreams in you to replace the old desires you once had for explicit materials. This is refilling. He will order your footsteps and point you in a new direction if you stay in tune with Him and His Word. When we do *not* have a close relationship with God, when we do not maintain regular communication with God through prayer, when we do not apply His Word to our lives, we become susceptible to the return of more impure spirits because our spiritual house is empty.

*****

God wants you to beat your porn habit. You're so precious to Him and your success is very important to Him (Jeremiah 29:11). God does not desire to condemn you for watching sexually explicit materials. He does not want you to feel so guilty that you reject His help and the assistance of others around you. At this very moment, He is fully aware of the spiritual attack that you face and has the power you need to abstain from pornography.

Ask God to remove impure spirits from your life and implement the three-step detoxification protocol (confess your secret, commit to abstain, and become accountable to another person). To maintain your abstinence, remember to launch an aggressive counter-attack powered by regular prayer, connecting with God's Word, and closely monitoring your triggers. When you bring all this together, you'll begin to notice a change in your thought patterns. Viewing and reading pornographic material will become less and less appealing as your spirit will begin to reject what your mind previously desired so much.

When you're in the trenches fighting hard to destroy the influences that impure spirits have over your life, don't shy away from friends or loved ones who can help you. This isn't the time to alienate yourself, even though you may experience an overwhelming urge to hide or retreat. Impure spirits desire to control your thoughts and behavior. They will always work hard to alienate you from the assistance of others.

Remain vigilant to avoid traps set by the Deceiver. This doesn't mean you should have fear of, or become overly obsessed with, Satan's works. Instead, operate with a heightened level of spiritual awareness. You will increase your ability to discern sneaky attacks as you become closer to God through prayer and reading Scriptures. Satan is the biggest and best liar of them all; therefore, know the promises of God as revealed through Scriptures so when you do hear Satan's lies (and yes, you'll hear them) you can disregard them as untrue.

God will *never* give up on you. His grace is sufficient for all things and covers you even if you stumble in your abstinence journey (2 Corinthians 12:9). He has the power to help you remove any impure spirits, and break any habitual sexual sin, including pornography consumption. ■

Chapter Nine

Parishioners Watch Too!

One day I was praying with my friend Catherine (who I affectionately call "Cat"). During this particular phone call we were praying for our married friends, including Cat and her husband.

"Cat, I love the relationship you have with your hubby," I said. "Of all my married friends, you guys seem to have figured it out."

"Thanks, girl," Cat said with a chuckle. "It's not always easy, but we do our best."

"No, I'm serious," I insisted. "You guys put God first in your marriage, you're active in your church, you're givers, and you both genuinely enjoy being around each other after all these years. That's hard to come by these days."

As we continued to chat, Cat asked, "So how's the book coming?"

"It's coming..." I replied sheepishly, knowing that I was currently in the throes of writer's block.

"You know," Cat shared, "Jess watches pornography sometimes. I'm not into it, but he does watch it occasionally."

"Really?" I inquired.

"Yeah, he doesn't watch all the time, but he watches. It's not a big deal to me," Cat said matter-of-factly.

I was surprised by the casual nature of Cat's revelation. How many other couples have comfortably integrated pornography into their bedrooms? And even more perplexing, how many *Christian* couples are engaged in this same practice? Does the formality of being married green-light a couple's experimentation with porn? Is marriage still considered sacred?

If asked, many would agree that certain practices, such as infidelity, can jeopardize the success of a marital union. With pornography, many couples are unwittingly engaging in these risky activities, just not in the traditional way we typically think of them. Consider the following prophetic Scripture that describes what our society will look like in the last days before the return of Christ:

> "For people will love only themselves and their money. They will be boastful and proud, scoffing at God, disobedient to their parents, and ungrateful. They will consider nothing sacred." (2 Timothy 3:2; NLT)

When I read this verse I was struck by the reference to considering "nothing sacred." The English word *sacred* is defined as "exclusively to one service or use." The Greek word for sacred is *hieros,* which is defined as "consecrated to God." Marriage is sacred because one is given exclusively to another and the union itself is consecrated to God.

When couples introduce pornography into their bedrooms and consume the sexual activities of others, the exclusivity bond between the husband and wife begins to weaken. Arousal develops, not from the caress of one spouse to another, but is generated by the images seen or the erotic text that is read. And while it's easy to assume that what we see and what we read cannot equate to an actual adulterous act, we must guard our minds against lustful intent because the Word of God tells us our sexual thoughts have the ability to render us guilty of adultery, even in the absence of physical contact (Matthew 5:28).

At the beginning of time, God fashioned Eve from Adam's bone:

> "Then the Lord God made a woman from the rib he had taken out of the man, and he brought her to the man. The man said, 'This is now bone of my bones

> and flesh of my flesh; she shall be called "woman," for she was taken out of man.'" (Genesis 2:22–23; NIV)

God did not create two helpmates for Adam, just one. God's original design for marriage is based on exclusivity, uniting two as one:

> "'For this reason a man will leave his father and mother and be united to his wife, and the two will become one flesh.' So they are no longer two, but one flesh. Therefore what God has joined together, let no one separate." (Mark 10:6–9; NIV)

Pornography undermines the Creator's plan for marriage. When women view sexual images or read erotic text, arousal and lustful thoughts are generated by the content consumed—not by their spouse. Even if the husband is the ultimate beneficiary of that desire, the sexual exclusivity of the marriage union is weakened. The Creator implores us to keep marriage sacred (Hebrews 13:4).

*****

Remember the television show *I Love Lucy*? Even today, Lucy's antics are hilarious to me and the show remains an enduring entertainment for our modern times. On the program, Lucy and Ricky were married, but the sexual intimacy of their marriage was not publically displayed (although they were married in real life too); in fact, the nighttime scenes showed them sleeping in two separate beds. Decades later, it's a different story. On television, in movies, and certainly in pornography, it's common to see people (married or not) engaged in sexual intercourse for public consumption.

The Scriptures say that we are to be imitators of God:

> "Imitate God, therefore, in everything you do, because you are his dear children." (Ephesians 5:1; NLT)

To imitate someone means to take on that person's characteristics—to talk like that person, behave like that person, to make the same type of decisions as that person. Because the Creator promotes exclusivity within marriage, I'm going to go out on a limb here and say that does not include the use of pornography; therefore, should we? Or have we ignored the Creator's direction on this subject? Is it no longer applicable in today's society? I believe it is.

The Scriptures warn us against loving what's popular as it relates to feelings of lust generated by what we see (1 John 2:15–16). I believe this includes the mainstreaming of porn and erotica for women. Justifying pornography consumption, even as a consenting act shared privately between a married couple, runs contrary to the Creator's plan for exclusivity within a marriage.

Silent Sermons

In 2004, the Indian Ocean was the epicenter of a massive earthquake that resulted in a deadly tsunami. This natural disaster stole hundreds of thousands of lives. For days, local and national news covered the tragic aftermath, broadcasting constant images of devastation and loss. Countries throughout the world united to pour in resources and aid in the recovery. Many of us, compelled to help, donated goods, contributed financial assistance, and prayed for the families affected by this tragedy. However, over time, the constant news reports began to fade, as did our sense of urgency in responding to the disaster. Before long, local news no longer carried the story. When we no longer saw the images of destruction and when our broadcasters stopped discussing this catastrophe, it slipped silently from our minds. We closed our wallets, stopped donating our goods, and forgot to pray for these countries, despite the lengthy clean-up and rebuilding process.

In our congregations, we've stopped discussing pornography consumption—actually, we never started. It's as if this issue doesn't exist within the four walls of the church. As a result, we fail to create environments that address this subject in a non-confrontational, non-judgmental way. On Sunday morning, there's no safe place to dialogue or to seek support in becoming porn-free, as many of our leaders resist teaching on this subject. Somehow there's a misconception that porn consumption, especially for women, is an issue from which the church is exempt, but consider that four out of ten women (42 percent) between the ages of 31 and 49 view pornography at least monthly. In addition, married women watch porn at the same level as unmarried women for this age category.[1]

Sexual immorality does not respectfully stop outside the front door of the church. No, it muscles its way in and sits in the pews with us every Sunday, satisfied that there are no aggressive campaigns to kick it out. When there is no dialogue about pornography consumption, we fall victim to the false belief that this is an activity others engage in—not Christians. When we stifle conversations in our Bible studies, in our prayer groups, and even in our youth ministries, we are in danger of drawing incorrect conclusions. Suddenly it's acceptable to justify porn use in the marriage bed. It becomes easy to adopt the mindset of our popular culture, which often glorifies the use of sexually explicit materials as a tool of liberation for women.

When we stopped discussing the 2004 tsunami, it was easy to assume that buildings were restored and there was no need for further assistance. In reality, coastal communities suffered for months with contaminated drinking water wells. Impoverished workers contended with an extensive and lengthy interruption of the local fishing industry, and thousands of families remained traumatized by the psychological and spiritual affects caused by the sudden deaths and incomplete burials of their loved ones.

The Creator desires that we expose those things that are done in darkness (Ephesians 5:8–13). The purpose of exposure is not to judge or condemn, rather, to bring light to that which causes us to stumble. Illumination helps us to evaluate those things we hold so tightly in the dark so that we see them for what they truly are. Often, they don't look as attractive as we originally perceived them to be.

Creating opportunities to openly discuss pornography attractions within the four walls of the church brings light to many who are suffering in darkness. The Creator's light allows us to have open conversations about the repercussions of pornography usage. This light is necessary to cultivate an atmosphere for change. Light reveals truth and helps create a safe environment to express challenges without fear of reprisal or judgment. When no light is brought to the dark, believers who struggle with porn pay the ultimate price. They continue to stumble in darkness, suffering silently.

I know pornography consumption is not an easy topic to discuss. It makes people uncomfortable, but that doesn't mean it shouldn't be broached. The message of pornography abstinence needs to be heard over and over to be effective. We must become more comfortable discussing this issue that impacts youth, men, and women. None of us is exempt.

*****

Many believers who struggle with pornography consumption fear the judgment of man. They seem to worry more about what others will think of them and less about God's instructions on this issue; however, the Creator reminds us:

> "Don't be bluffed into silence by the threats of bullies. There's nothing they can do to your soul, your core being. Save your fear for God, who holds your entire life—body and soul—in his hands." (Matthew 10:28; The Message Bible)

Whoa! Every time I read that passage it reminds me how dangerous it is to ignore God's Word and allow others to justify my sin. In our quest to be politically correct and inclusive of every whim, we've devalued the strength of the Creator and the mightiness of His character. So often we're more concerned about what our friends and family may think about us instead of what the Creator has proclaimed. We consciously (or unconsciously) tailor our behavior to meet others' approval and avoid their judgment. In reality, the *only* judgment we need be concerned with is that of the Creator.

We can find relief from life's pressures when we yield our will to the Creator who says:

> "Come to me, all of you who are weary and carry heavy burdens, and I will give you rest. Take my yoke upon you. Let me teach you, because I am humble and gentle at heart, and you will find rest for your souls. For my yoke is easy to bear, and the burden I give you is light." (Matthew 11:28–30; NLT)

The Creator doesn't seek to put us in bondage or enslave us with a long list of things we cannot do. Our mainstream culture often views the Creator's direction as restrictive and unnecessary, evidenced by the growing acceptance of pornography as a form of entertainment, despite its negative themes. Conformation to what's popular can put us at odds with the Creator's design for our lives. A constant struggle between doing what is "in" and doing what we were created to do can cause discontentment. It's like swimming upstream against the flow of a strong current. When we work against what we were created to be, we live restless, unfulfilled lives.

Purpose Without Porn

The Creator has given you a purpose to fulfill on this earth. This purpose is good and provides tremendous benefit to you, those around you, and oftentimes those you may never meet personally. Even if you don't know your purpose, you still have one. Even if you think you're too old (or too young) to discover your purpose, you still have one.

Maintaining an intimate relationship with the Creator is essential to discovering and fulfilling your purpose. The further you are from Him, the more difficult it becomes to hear His gentle voice that provides direction for your life. Imagine being lost at sea with a boat, oars, food, but no compass. How would you find your way home? In the absence of direction, confusion, hopelessness, and doubt creep in. The Creator gives us direction to achieve the purpose He has planned.

About fourteen years ago, I began to feel a strong desire to start a business. I had been working professionally for years and had recently been laid off from a well-paying, exciting job. I began my job search, optimistic about finding another company to call home. After months of full-time job hunting and multiple, promising interviews, I had no offers. Visions of starting my own business began to consume me. I had never thought about entrepreneurship, and yet, here were these "feelings" propelling me forward to try something that I had never done before. However, dogged by fear, I continued to look for employment, unsuccessfully.

This was confusing, as I knew my work experience was marketable. *Why couldn't I land a job?* Out of desperation, I developed a business plan to start my own company. The ideas flowed naturally as I clearly began to understand the type of enterprise I would operate. Today I am the owner of a successful and thriving consulting firm.

Although I didn't realize it at the time, it was God's plan for me to start a business. This was His purpose for me, even though I resisted heavily at first. The job searching that I insisted on resulted in continuous confusion and disappointment; however, when I began to operate in God's purpose, my life came into focus and I understood exactly what direction to travel in. The benefits of operating in God's purpose aren't exclusively for me. By starting my own company, I've been able to offer long-term employment for others and I believe the work of my team has had a positive impact on the lives of many clients we've served over the years.

Satan doesn't want you to follow the Creator's direction, and he definitely doesn't want you to fulfill your purpose. He has attempted to interrupt God's plan since Adam and Eve's temptation. So what does he do? He distracts you with all sorts of inconspicuous activities. Things like busyness, selfish ambition, excessive working, and unhealthy relationships will all get the job done. Viewing pornography is another distraction that will shove you off course. Continuous digestion of sexually explicit images stymies the relationship that you have with the Creator; when you're distant, when you have difficulty hearing His voice, your purpose gets contaminated. When this intimate relationship with the Creator is diminished, it becomes more difficult to discover and fulfill God's purpose.

What has pornography stopped you or someone you know from achieving? Freedom from feelings of guilt or shame? A closer relationship with your spouse? Clarity of thought to accomplish your goals? Restoration of a damaged relationship? What dreams and desires have you compromised because of your preoccupation with porn? What purpose have you aborted because of your pornography habit?

Scripture tells us that we are equipped to live a godly life:

> "By his divine power, God has given us everything we need for living a godly life. We have received all of this by coming to know him, the one who called us to himself by means of his marvelous glory and excellence." (2 Peter 1:3; NLT)

We've all been divinely created to live a life committed to the Creator's great plan. We're hardwired to His specifications. When we cultivate a relationship with the Creator, all circuits are go! Everything about us—the things we say and the things we do—begins to operate in harmony with the Creator. We should endeavor to honor His plan for our lives, not because our parents say so, not because our pastors say so, but because our Creator, who is so faithful, who loves us unconditionally, who has rescued us time and time again from our own folly, says so. For the plans that He has for us will not cause us harm, but instead are designed to bring prosperity (Jeremiah 29:11).

Living a godly life requires us to have a relationship with the Creator through personal prayer time. It also requires that we study Scripture so that we understand His essence, His principles, and the purpose for which He has called us to fulfill in this lifetime. When we decide to care more about the Creator's plan than what's trending, and when we develop the courage to stand for our beliefs no matter how unpopular they may be, we experience a level of freedom that brings the ultimate peace only the Creator can provide!

If you've allowed your pornography consumption to compromise your purpose, take comfort in knowing that you have a restart available with the Creator. Start today! It's never too late to get back on track. Remember, God can do all things and His purposes cannot be thwarted (Job 42:2)! ■

Endnotes

1. The website of the Proven Men Ministry, "2014 Porn Survey," Barna Group, accessed December 20, 2014, http://www.provenmen.org/2014pornsurvey/

Appendix

Accountability Software Providers

X3Watch	www.x3watch.com
Covenant Eyes	www.covenanteyes.com
Internet safety	www.internetsafety.com
Integrity Online	www.integrity.com

Accountability Partner Resources

Coming Clean: Overcoming Lust Through Biblical Accountability. Free E-Book for Christian Accountability Partners, http://www.covenanteyes.com/accountability-partner-ebook/

Open: What Happens When You Get Real, Get Honest, and Get Accountable, by Craig Gross (Thomas Nelson, 2013)

Recovery Programs and Online Support Groups

X3Pure XXX Church	www.x3pure.com
Dirty Girls Ministry	www.dirtygirlsministry.com

Additional Book Resources

Dirty Girls Come Clean, by Crystal Renaud (Moody Publishers, 2011)

Healing Your Marriage When Trust is Broken, by Cindy Beall (Harvest House Publishers, 2011)

Naked Surrender: Coming Home to Our True Sexuality, by Andrew Comiskey (Inter-varsity Press, 2010)

Healing Wounds of Sexual Addiction, by Mark R. Laaser (Zondervan, 2004)

www.girlswatchtoo.com